Lanzarote Motor tour

Contents

Introduction

Lanzarote is an island with other-worldly wonders, missed by far too many visitors. Coach tours help but cannot reach the more obscure locations that will thrill you. This is an attempt to guide you to the most exciting venues.

If you were willing to walk a little you would see even more. I would point you to *Walking in Lanzarote, Lambert and Wheeler*; probably the most adventurous walking guide that you will find. https://www.goodreads.com/book/show/34260379-walking-in-lanzarote

Anyway, if you want to see wonders, this route could be driven in a busy day (*just about*) or (*more sensibly*) in snippets over several days. There are so many marvels that are never seen by most of visitors; try this tour and prepare yourself!

The photo set amounts to a picture-tour of the island, but you'll take far better ones for yourself and I'll be pleased to see any that you want to share. nwheeler@brookes.ac.uk

The journey is described as a circuit, from the centre to the Southern tip, on to the Northernmost point and back to the centre. Really, of course, you can start and finish anywhere. For convenience the trip is described as though it is a single journey, but of course it will take it in slices over many days. We think that it would amuse you for the best part of a week picking up section by section and exploring the amazing places en-route. If you also walk the recommended walks it will keep you happy for about year.

Note: This text is offered on the inventive new 'Createspace' Publishing platform for two reasons:

1) *The costs to the reader are far lower than traditional publishing houses.*
2) *It is easy to update and improve the work; the text is continually under review. To this end the readers and the authors form a community to develop the work. As a reader, you are invited to email suggestions to nwheeler@brookes.ac.uk Contributions may be simple 'typo' alerts, corrections to detail, new areas to cover, etc. All contributors are acknowledged in the print and E-Book versions, with our thanks.*

On Accommodation

There is a fine array of accommodation options to be found on the island at very modest prices. Large centres like Costa Teguise on the West coast or Playa Blanca in the South offer beaches, bars and shops galore, if that is your bag.

Personally we like something quieter and more intimate, and the best village we have found is Charco Del Paulo. Look at http://www.nudelanza.com/ for a fine array of villas and apartments, many opening right onto the sand. There are sea swimming areas, three bars, a supermarket and general *peace&quiet*. Many walks start and end here. True, they can be a bit casual about wearing clothes but you can dress as minimally or modestly as your taste requires and nobody will turn a hair. Enquire after the fabulously good value Apartamento Del Vista. If your Spanish is really good, you might stay in Haria, which is the finest of Island towns.

On Car hire.

To have a car on Lanzarote is essential. Hire is inexpensive, often less than the cost of hotel transfers and there is so much magic to be seen on this eccentric island that you just have to get out and explore. The roads are very good and the traffic fairly light.

Carry your driving licence, passport and insurance on every journey. Wear good shoes and your shirt. To fail on any of these rules carries a fine.

Coach tours exist, and these are good, but their schedule will not match yours, they can only show you 'Tourist hotspots' with big carparks and whenever you arrive somewhere it's crowded because *'a coach has just pulled in'*. They can only show you the mainstream places rather than the more obscure ones. Eg they take you to plush wineries, rather than the little artisan ones. They have to take you to specific main road bars rather than the quiet tapas bars.

There are endless car hire offers in Lanzarote, but you should beware of two considerations.

1) It is often a mistake to hire through the airline. The deal may be OK, but it may mean that half of your aeroplane has booked with the same provider and then queues for that one desk will be far longer than any of the others.
2) Some of the providers will offer a low headline price and then make up the price with a very hard sell on insurance top up and then charge you even more on returning the car for a mythical refuelling . (Nothing said at the time – just an unexpected charge on your card when you get home).

We find *Plus Cars* to be good. The base price matches the others but there is no additional charge for insurance or petrol, so you know where you stand. Go to: http://www.nudelanza.com/car-hire.html.

On flora and fauna

Far more grows on the island than people imagine; the soil is very much more fertile that it appears and water can be taken from the humid atmosphere by cunning deployment of pecon. Farming includes: Lanzarote palms, grapes, figs, olives, oranges, lemons, almonds, potatoes, leeks, onions, peas, strawberries, melons, chillies and peppers, etc *(and etc!)*. The fresh food offer with minimal food miles is quite remarkable.

Wild plants include a wealth of cacti, geraniums, sedum, nicotiana, and many more. After a little rain, the island hosts masses of wild-flower meadows.

In the sky, there are hawks, kestrels, buzzards, Bustards, ravens, little egrets, choughs, sparrows, hoopoes, doves, pipits, chaffinches, goldcrests, canaries and more. **On the ground** there are lizards and their heavier cousins, the geckoes. These will eat banana from your hand in many of the beachside pods. There are mice, rabbits and hedgehogs everywhere if you look for the signs. **In the sea** there is a fine array of fish. They too eat from your hand.

On Places to visit

Sociedads
Lanzarote's Sociedads (*AKA Teleclub and Centro Social Cultural, CSC*) offer good local dining and more, if you can find them. See: *Sociedads of Lanzarote. Wheeler*

Be'lens
Look out for Christmas Be'lens Nativity/model villages.

Group tickets
For us, the island is unrivalled in the world for landscape and artefacts and it rewards every trip out by car, if you know where to look. The following is a basic list and we generally don't like visitors to leave until they have experienced each of them at least once. As an economy, it is possible to buy a batch of tickets allowing entry to up to five of these remarkable locations at a significant reduction – and well worth it.

The Cactus Garden.

Guatiza on the LZ1 hosts this amazing garden. The layout is extremely clever and the collection of cacti breath-taking. A look inside the windmill is also a privilege. Nearby, in Mala, there is the renowned Arepera Restaurant and across the main road from there it is possible to see *(from the road and for free)* an almost better cactus garden; check out both on one trip.

Jamos Del Aqua.
This staggering cave system made splendid by Caesar Manrique is on the LZ1 Orzola Road is a most amazing experience, not to be missed, but frequently to be repeated *(we do, anyway)*.

Cueva los Verda.
Another cave system, actually linked to Jamos *Del Aqua,* being part of the same lava tube, is

Just off the LZ1 Orzola road on the LZ204. This is a very different more natural, but equally amazing experience, also not to be missed.

The Mirador Del Rio.
This Mirador (viewing point) is near Orzola on the North-West extreme of the island and is a magnificent Cesar Monrique construction. After enjoying the building and the view for a bit, I have to marvel at the engineers who built it.

Salinas de Janubio
On the South-West coast, not far from Playa Blanca is an active salt pan, where hills of salt are to be seen. There is an intriguing system of canals designed to take sea water and fill each bay where it is left to evaporate and the salt collected by hand. This pan is still said to produce 15,000 tonnes of salt per year, but that is less than a third of production of this industry in its heyday. Before, refrigeration, the salt was a major industry for the island, being used to preserve fish. Today's harvest is exported. *(There being little need to salt the roads in Lanzarote.)*

Fuego de Timanfaya.
The famous, Fire Mountain, on the west of the island is a true spectacle. Ideally visit at opening time (10-am) because the access is narrow and traffic builds up later in the day. The crust is thin and ground too hot in places to walk. See geysers, barbeque meat over the hot ground and take the bus tour over a landscape that you will never forget.

Los Hevidaros
This is a fabulous spectacle on the West coast, on the LZ702 that sees crashing waves assault the cliff and pass under natural arches and you can watch it all from walkways and galleries built into and on top of the cliff. This is unlike anything else on the island. Like so much else that is good on Lanzarote the layout was designed by Cesar Monrique.

El Golfo.
On the West coast, on the LZ702 lies this is a charming village and a short walk *(No, Really; it is a very short walk)* over a hill takes you to an emerald green inland lake. There are a few nice restaurants, too.

The two homes of Cesar Monrique,
Both of Monrique's homes were donated to become museums. One is in Haria and the other (The Foundation) is near to Tahiche. Both need to be seen *(to be believed)*. They represent eccentricity at its most brilliant.

Lag Omar,
In Nazaret near Teguise, signed from the LZ10, Lag Omar is a home built by Cesar Monrique for Omar Sharif. It is set into a quarry rock face with external staircases linking normal rooms, each build into a cave. The surreal placing of (for example) modern kitchen fittings into a cave is something that will blow you away.

Castillo Santa Barbara

Is a castle near to the old capital town, Teguise, where it was once necessary to retreat from pirates; a dramatic building with far reaching views. A few minutes' study here will give a real insight into the lives of islanders plagued by pirates.

Wine and cheese, unspoiled Bodega

Leaving Orzola heading South-Westerly on the LZ201, you may be lucky enough to see a hand painted sign on your right for this Mexican style farm. Drive in for charming wine and cheese tasting in a building that might be a living museum. This is much more 'real' (*not to say cheaper*) than the big commercial wineries that you would find in La Garia.

Lanzarote a Caballo

To be found on the LZ2 near Playa del Carmen the Lanzarote a Caballo offers pony and camel riding in a very nice and informal way. You can ride camels at the Fuego de Timanfaya, but that is a little *coach-trippy*. For a far more personal experience riding on a saddle not in a basket, go to Cabello. If you prefer, they would arrange horse riding, buggies, trikes, and even paint ball (*if you must*). 10:00 AM to 05:30 PM.

Beaches

Playa de Papagayo, near Playa Blanca is a great place to play in the waves on a sandy beach and affords plenty of scope for sandcastles. One beach is clothed; one beach is naturist. You can take your pick.

Playa de Famara on the West coast is a long sandy beach great for views and sun with a naturist tolerance, but although there are surfers galore, it is not recommended for swimming as the currents are dangerous and drownings are recorded almost every year.

Orzola and Isla Graciosa. At the northern extremity of the island, on the LZ1, Orzola has the ferry to Isla Graciosa which has some very fine beaches. Heading North on the LZ1, approaching Orzola there are several small isolated sandy places by the water with parking allowing secluded bathing and Orzola itself has a good safe beach.

Towns

See: splendid Haria, Medieval Teguise, charming Yaiza, Uga & Femes if nowhere else, but really the style of house and their general unspoiled nature makes all of the old towns a treat to visit.*(The new ones, of course, are a matter of taste.)*

Markets

Arrecife   Monday to Friday:

Recova Market 9am to 2pm - Fresh local produce and local artisan craft shops
Fish Market - 9am to 1pm - Local fish and sea food caught fresh each day

Playa Blanca   Wednesday & Saturday
Marina Rubicon - 9.30am to 1.30pm - About 30 stalls with crafts, jewellery, arts and books

Costa Teguise   Friday
Pueblo Marinero - 6pm to 10pm - Small and busy evening market, mainly crafts and souvenirs, great atmosphere.

Haria   Saturday

Artisan Market - 10am to 2.30pm - Various stalls with handmade crafts and artwork, some local produce stalls, a bit quirky and different.

Tias   Saturday
Recova Market - 9am to 2pm - Small market with local goods and produce

Mancha Blanca   Sunday
Local agricultural market- 9am to 2pm - The best island market for local produce and fresh fruit and vegetables.

Teguise   Sunday
Island market - 9am to 2pm - The biggest market in Lanzarote selling everything; arts, jewellery, clothes, bags, linen and leather goods.

The Drive: Start

We begin at Arrecife and take the LZ3 (Circumvolution) around Arrecife until joining the LZ2, towards Playa Blanca.

Tias and Mancher

We pass through Tias, where you cannot fail to be amazed by the flintstone development on your left.

Tias is a pleasant small town that you may want to favour with a few minutes tour. *Like every place we'll meet stop and walk.*

Puerto Del Carmen

Signed on the Left, is Puerto del Carmen, a dramatic and busy seaside town. This is not unlike a large, old-fashioned, English seaside town, with a long, manic, seafront parade of bars, hotels, casinos and night clubs. Nice beaches and sea views.

Puerto Calero and Puerto Quemada

The LZ2 continues through Mancher and soon we are offered a turning on the left for *Puerto Calero* which is a very pleasant little beach village with a fine array of restaurants. Now, that's more like it! This justifies a few minutes consideration. Stop, look and walk.

Returning to and continuing on the LZ2 we are offered *Puerto Quemada*, another very nice beach village with restaurants. (There's a fine *Lambert and Wheeler* walk along the cliff from here.)

Lanzarote Caballo

The next roundabout is the Caballo, offering the best camel-ride experience on the island and also pony trecks and a range of road and of-road vehicles. This centre is worth a few minutes if just to see the impressive array of animals.

There is also a bar and playground.

Femes

Shortly after Caballo, we reach a large roundabout with very large camel statues where we take photos and then follow the LZ702, South, towards Playa Blanca.

The first

town is *Cacitas de Femes*, achieving world-wide renown for its eccentric garden. Anybody you talk to, anywhere in the world, says the same thing,

'Oh yes, Femes, I've been there, it's where they have a helicopter in the garden!'

There are a good many of these *'eccentric art installations'* in gardens all over the island. Sadly, not everyone is the next Manrique, but this particular garden is fun! (and photogenic).

Pressing on, you reach *Femes* which is very pleasant, having the eponymous Femes restaurant/bar, which offers a fine stew at a very modest price. Femes merits a few minutes exploration and the view from the Mirador by the church is dramatic, showing the island a far as Playa Blanca and beyond to Fuerteventura. There are many fine long and short Lambert & Wheeler walks to be had from here.

There is a goat farm up the dirt track to the left of the main road, opposite the eponymous bar, where you can mingle with adult and kid goats and get a fine view back over the village nestling against the mountains. Park by the church of the bar and cross the road to climb this short track to goggle at the view both East and West from the saddle in the mountain.

Playa Blanca

Leaving Femes you drop dramatically and steeply down from the mountain, taking the first exit from the roundabout crossing the Rubicon Plain to reach Playa Blanca. Just before reaching the town, there is a roundabout and taking a left turn onto a good quality dirt-track, takes you to Papagayo Beach. In fact there are a series of lovely sandy beaches, there. At the end of the track there is a parking area giving access to the beaches. Starting at the farthest away

to your left (Southernmost) the beach is clothed, the next is naturist, then next seems to be mixed. On the dirt-track keep the speed very low and you should have no trouble. If the *boy-racers* dash past you then ignore them, just think about the damage they are doing to their tyres. Don't damage your tyres with speedy driving as that is about the only thing for which all of the car hire firms will charge you.

After you take this beach detour, return from Papagayo to re-join the main road into Playa Blanca. Explore the town if you need a meal or would like to admire the well-developed water front. If you're not sold on the tourist development towns then just loop around to your right and join the LZ701 to La Hoya.

La Hoya and the Salinas de Janubio

On the North coast, La Hoya has the most intricate Salt Pans on the island. It is claimed that the island once produced 45,000-tonnes of salt in a year, primarily for salting fish and meat for passing sailing ships. The advent of deep-freeze preservation has reduced this, but these Salinas still reckon to produce around 15,000-tonnes of salt in a year. Take a few minutes to identify the various canals and sluices by which sea water is channelled into the many salt pans, closed off and left to

dry. The intricacy of this design would make Heath Robinson proud.

Los Hervideros

Continue on the LZ703 until you see parking on your Left for *Los Hervideros*. These are a series of rock faces and caves with fabulous walkways (*designed by Cesar Manrique, of course*) set into the sea where the waves crash with the most dramatic effect. This is a location *not to be missed* whatever else you do. If you happen to coincide with a coach, give it a minute, they never stay for long.

El Golfo

Continuing on the LZ703 you reach El Golfo which is a fine little seaside village with good range of restaurants and is the base for a fine Lambert and Wheeler walk, *(of course)*.

Parking on the left as you enter the village you will see a short trail to the South which takes you over the hill to a beach and an amazing emerald inland lake. This is a consequence of the unusual salts in the volcanic rock. For very little money you will be offered some fascinating rocks. Walk around the village before deciding which café/bar deserves your patronage.

Timanfaya and Montana del Fuego lava fields

From here take the LZ704 to Yaiza, a pleasant little town. Park up and explore for a while.

From here take the LZ67 into the lava fields, *another place absolutely not to be missed.* Take a few moments to marvel about how this road was built in terrain too rough even to walk on. Drive, mesmerised, until you find the camel park on your left. From here you can take a camel ride into the sand dunes, which is good, but not half as good as the rides you could take from *The Caballo,* above. The camel trains are a thing to see, though, so pull in and explore. It is usually OK to pet the camels. They are surprisingly endearing animals.

Continuing, through this surreal scenery, you soon reach the *Montana del Fuego* (Fire Mountain) on your left. There are times when this is a busy centre, so a little planning is no bad thing. Ideally get here early morning shortly after they open (at 9am), and not at the weekend. This is a little touristy, but there is nowhere like it, so a visit and a ride on their tour bus is an absolute must; an experience that you will never forget. *Another place absolutely not to be missed.*

Watch geysers from hot rocks; cook chicken over hot rocks; see twigs spontaneously ignite. Don't walk on the sand, it would cook your feet!

And then the bus trip through the lava field is too dramatic to describe.

After the *Montana del Fuego* and before you reach Mancha Blanca, there is a small museum (visitor centre) on the left which gives an idea of the importance of camels to the island, well worth a few minutes.

This road then takes us to Mancha Blanca

Mancha Blanca

Mancha Blanca is a very pleasant village with a fine church to explore and a very good and inexpensive Sunday flower, fruit & vegetable market.

Unsurprisingly, perhapse, we have a very good Lambert & Wheeler walk starting from Mancha Blanca.

La Geria

Take the LZ56, South, out of Mancha Blanca. Just before the junction with the LZ30, see Montana Cuervo on you left. A very short and easy walk will put you in the basin of this fantastic volcano. Only a short stroll and a quite spiritual experience.

Continue down the LZ56 and turn Right onto the LZ30. This road takes you through the Major wine region to the pleasant town of Uga. The these endless rows of circular 'pods' are worth a while's study. The volcanic rock makes an individual windbreak for each plant as well as providing a surface upon which dew collects and runs down to irrigate the plant.

There are bodegas, here, where wine can be sampled and purchased. There are some that will have a good display to explain the viniculture in greater detail. These are quite grand facilities and priced accordingly. For a more down-to earth version see *Bodega Los Almacenes* near *Ye*, below.

Uga, is a pleasant town well worth e few minutes, walking around. In particular find

the large hole beside the market. Try to figure or what it is/was. *(And consider the wondrous Lambert & Wheeler walks starting at Uga.)*

Return up the LZ30 al of the way until reaching the *Monumento el Campesino* on the junction between LZ30 and LZ20. The *Monumento el Campesino* is a Cesar Manrique piece to honour the island's workers. Park and explore; there is far more to be seen here than at first appears.

Famara

From the monumento, take the LZ20, West, to *Tiagua*, and then take the LZ401 through *Soo* and La *Caleta* to *Famara*. Each is a pleasant place with shops and restaurants, and each ought to be experienced on foot. However, for the best beach continue to Famara. This is a fine place with good facilities, mostly selling surfing gear and bars and a Sociedad (Look for the CSC sign). The road runs West, frequently covered in wind-swept sand dunes and circumnavigates a regimented chalet development, known as The Norwegian Village.

The track follows the beach for some way, with parking all along. It is worth a few minutes to watch the sea and the display of surfing skills, but more dramatic is the cliff on the other side of the road. Close scrutiny may even enable you to pick out the Mirador on the cliff, from which you will look down onto the beach later. *(Several fine L&W walks!)*

Teguise

From Famara, take the LZ402 towards Teguise and turn Left, West, on reaching the LZ30. Teguise was

originally the capital city before that role was taken over by Arrecife. This is quite a grand place, with a cathedral, some fine old, medieval streets and buildings and is well worth taking a good while to walk around and explore. There are plenty of fine café/bars for tapas and one or two good galleries. There's a beautiful Sociedad, but we've never found it open!

Nazaret and Lag Omar

From here a detour back down the LZ10 and branching off to the left, would take you to the pretty but normal enough town of Oasis de Nazaret. Here you could find the *far-from-normal: Lag Omar*, which is a home built into a quarry face by Cesar Manrique for Omar Sharif.

Return to Teguise, on the LZ10

Castillo Santa Barbara

From Teguise, the LZ10 North takes you towards the fine town of Haria.

As you Leave Teguise, *Castillo Santa Barbara,* is a splendid defensive position visible up a good track on the right.

This is well worth visiting. *(And part of a L&W walk!)*

Even if you don't go into the castle it is still worth driving up the track to admire the fortifications from the outside and appreciate the view that made this such a good defensive point against pirates.

The island had many years of trouble with pirates and this made a good secure place into which to withdraw.

Ermita de las Nieves

Returning to the LZ10, and proceeding West, takes you through the quite lush Los Valles *(...of the thousand palms)*, past the Parque Eolico, with its windmills visible from anywhere on the island and eventually down a zig-zag road into Haria.

Before the steep zig-zag descent into Haria, look for a left turn signed *Ermita de la Nieves* (roughly 'Chapel of snow'); usually the coldest spot on the island. Follow the distance and park at the chapel. From spectacular cliff, from where you can see Famara beach, far below, and Isla The chapel is charming and the area fine,

road for a short here stroll towards the the full length of Graciosa to the North. so spare it a little time.

Penas del Cache

We *return by a different route (Mat II:12);* take the left fork just back from the chapel and pass beneath the 'golf ball' military observatory before returning to the LZ10. Immediately before reaching the

LZ10, there is a track to the Left which can be reasonably safely traversed if you take it slowly. Follow this around to the right passing a farm with goats, cattle and chickens. *(If you don't see the*

animals you'll smell them). This opens up onto a car park with picknick and barbeque stands and a most impressive view back over Famara beach, in one direction and Isla Graciosa in the other.

Miradors

Return down the track turn Left onto the LZ10 and park on the right of the LZ10, immediately opposite the exit from your track and walk a few steps South, to a Mirador over a valley and be prepared to be amazed by the view.

Drive North to the first car park on the right where there is a large café/bar offering coffee, Estrella beer and fine snacks at good prices. This is not a good use of such a splendid location, but we must have a drink and gaze over a different valley, seeing Tabayesco and then Guatiza in the distance. The road to Tabayesco is clearly visible just below, with a house built into the precipitous roadside. One story high on the roadside and three high on the back. The food is good and the beer cold. *'Dos jarra pour favour'.* The service is good, but the nice man behind the bar is another one who repeatedly looks at me and my (undeniably female) companion and assumes that what I really want is to order a 1½-pints; not 2-pints; surely for a girl ½-pint is plenty!

> *Now, I mention in the spirit of friendship - Don't tell Emma that she is a girl and therefore can only manage a ½-pint of Cerveza. Not if you want to like to keep your gonads inside your scrotum. This fellow has done it on more than one occasion. Once more and I will not be responsible for the consequences.*

Haria

Exit the car park and turn right (North) negotiating the chicanes cautiously as you drop down the mountain all of the way to Haria. As you go down, the view is remarkable. Notice the intriguing paths leaving the road on Left and Right; these are sometimes called the Pilgrim Path or the Hidden Path and are the subject of a number of truly splendid L&W walks.

Haria is a fine little town having splendidly attractive, modest houses and a few very grand ones, several of which are long abandoned.

(Established buildings being abandoned can often be as a result of distributed ownership. In the absence of a will, a considerable number of relatives can find themselves as part owners and every one of them must agree to the sale and then attend the Notary in person in order to make a sale possible. Half-built houses are more often abandoned because they did not enjoy planning consent. Sometimes residents get away with unofficial development but for others the police enforce a hold on the work and the shell stands abandoned for many years before it is removed.)

Haria has a range of artisan shops, a fine market square with a splendid Sociedad at the Church end and much (MUCH) more. Not to be missed is the final home of Cesar Manrique, gifted to the island as a museum and a most amazing piece of eccentric architecture. Still just as he left it.

Form Haria, there are a good number of L&W walks to suit every level of ability.

Maguez

The LZ201 goes uphill, North through Haria, from the Market Square, to Maguez. These two small towns are almost contiguous. Maguez is another pleasant town, having a few nice small café/bars and merits a stroll. Los Helchos mountains to the left, West, are the site of a fine L&W walk.

And then the LZ201 takes us towards Ye.

Mirador de Guinate

Leaving Maguez, you will soon see the sign for The Parque Tropical, (closed at the time of writing), on your left. Turn in to that road and continue to the very end to see the Mirador de Guinate. This offers another magnificent view of Isla Graciosa and Famara Beach. *(And a couple of splendid walks!)* Also a very nice Sociedad.

Guatifay

Guatifay is another '*not-to-be-missed*' sight. Return to the LZ201 and turn Left (North) until you see a parking area on the Left with a palm tree. From this point it is OK to slowly traverse the dirt-track passing a house on the Left and park bedside a white house on the Right. From here, take a very short

walk to the cliff edge. The path follows the cliff edge and offers possible the finest scenery on the island. Traverse the path (carefully!) as far as you see fit before retracing your steps or looping back to the car. If you don't fancy the dirt-track, then park under the palm tree and walk the short extra distance to the white house on the right and from there strike off to your left to reach the cliff edge. *(There are two very fine L&W walks which take in this area.)*

Guinate Cliff

Return to the LZ201 turning Left (North) until by a bus stop you see a Left turn, LZ202, just before reaching the town of Ye. This road takes you through some very dramatic lava shapes in the midst of which you see a stone paved track to your Left. Follow this to a parking place. From here walk along the path and

observe a breath-taking stairway down the cliff.

(Naturally, this is the subject of one of our walks). Also take a moment to marvel at the shapes created by lava upheaval all along this paved track.

Mirador Del Rio

Seen enough miradors? You haven't seen this one! Another *'not-to-be-missed'* sight.

Returning down the stone paved track through the lava shapes, turn Left and follow the narrow LZ202 around the cliff edge. This is a tight road, but has stone walls and ample passing places so is an easy drive and offers ever changing views to delight and impress. This road ends at the Mirador Del Rio which is (another) Cesar Manrique creation built onto the edge of the cliff and must be seen for the wonders of the building itself as well as the view it exploits.

Having enjoyed the building it is worth a stroll back along the road by which you came here, to better appreciate the spectacle.

Ye and the Montana Corona

Return to Ye, by the LZ202, rather than the road that brought you here. Park by the church and explore the village. In particular, look at the Montana corona behind the village. (Of course the subject of a couple of fine L&W walks). As a very short trek, there is a path from Ye high street to the volcano, which would be well worth the effort. You can walk right up to the edge of this (long extinct) volcano and look far down the precipitous rock face into the basin. If

you are intrepid enough, you can even walk down a track to the basin floor from where the experience is almost mystical.

Orzola and Bodega Los Almacenes

Take the LZ201 out of Ye and be ready to turn Left onto the LZ204 for Orzola. Before reaching the turning, look for a hand-painted sign on the Right, selling wine. Turn up this drive and park near the building and explore. The farm house is brilliant, with all sorts of water catching channels and forms a defensible area that recalls Yul Brynner in 'The Magnificent Seven'. There is an outside cellar selling excellent wines, cheeses and sauces at very reasonable prices; you are invited to try each before buying. This feels so much more 'real' than the bodegas at La Geria and at very much better prices. Rarely found by tourists.

Return to the LZ201 and turn Left onto the LZ204 to reach Orzola. This is a busier town because it hosts the ferry to the Island Isla Graciosa. *(Sounds like a Hogwarts spell, but if it is I don't know what it does)*. It has a nice beach magnificently nestled under very sheer cliffs. There is a Sociedad and restaurants aplenty. There is also a good supermarket and cash point. *(From here there are two very gentle ½-hour L&W*

walks.) Take the LZ204 to reach Orzola drive into the high street. Immediately after the supermarket, turn Left and head down the dirt-track to the beach car park at the far end. This track is safe enough, but go very slowly and ignore the 'boy-racers'.

At the parking area, there is a very nice sandy beach. This is worthy of a careful paddle, but not ideal for swimming as there can be aggressive under-currents. To the right of the beach, South, there is a remarkable green area criss-crossed with paths.

Returning to the high street, turn left and take the next left, Calle Lajail, to the car park at the end of the road. From here, head straight towards the water. Wonder through sand paths between madly eccentric lava rock natural sculptures and carefully approach the water line. Here the effect is dramatic and there are rock pools to admire.

Making your way past the harbour, you find more little side streets beside the water with attractive apartments with a nice safe inlet for a (*swimsuited*) dip. Finally, explore the bars and shops and then you have done justice to this pretty little town.

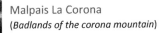

Malpais La Corona
(*Badlands of the corona mountain*)

Take the LZ1 out of Orzola and pass through the lava fields created by the Corona mountain behind you. Take a moment to admire this dramatic mountain. These fields are quite different again from any others you have seen and occasionally sport some significant greenery. To the left of the road there are a series of beaches, with parking places and these merit exploration (*Of course there is a very fine walk, too...*) Some of these little beaches are quite busy and others more remote where bathers are less fussy about swimsuits if you need to cool off.

Jameos Del Agua
Return to the LZ1, continuing south, and this incredible structure appears on your Left; it is unmissable. These caves were formed by lava tunnels and the *visit is a magical experience.*

The cave was magnificently developed by Cesar Manrique.

Cueva De Las Verdes
Exiting Jameos Del Agua, cross over the LZ1 and take the road West in order to find Cueva De Las Verdes. Another cave, to be sure, but 100% different, being far more natural, and *another trip that must not be missed.*

Continuing along the LZ1, takes you to firstly Punta Mujeres and then Arrieta. Each is a pleasant seaside development worthy of a stroll and a waterside drink. The garage at Arietta

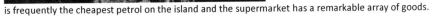

is frequently the cheapest petrol on the island and the supermarket has a remarkable array of goods.

Punta Mujeres and Arrieta

These two villages seem unexciting if you stay on the LZ roads. However, if you park and wonder on foot, there are charming houses and streets. In **Arrieta** it is not possible to walk along the water front because buildings extend right to the waterfront and often over the sea. Several of the café bars extend over the water offering a very impressive dining experience.

Punta Mujeres, is more untouched than Arrieta, with older buildings and extensive fishing. It allows

access to the water for most of its length, and there are several natural tidal pools, enhanced by good steps, making bathing a very good experience.

There is a *'Pill-Box'* defensive station, reminding the historically minded that these islands occupy important strategic positions.

Mala, Charco Del Paulo & The Cactus Garden

Leave the LZ10 at the next exit, signed Mala, which has a nice church, a supermarket and three very fine Bars.

The Sociedad (Cantina de Mala) offers fine Tapas and drinks at very pleasing prices, as Sociedads always do. The Arepera serves beer so cold that ice forms in the head, and the food is excellent. The Don Quixote offers food and drink to a very satisfactory standard.

As a short detour: take the road opposite the Arepera and Don Quixote to the West and circle around to your right. This will eventually take you back to the High Street. On this loop you will see on your right a most amazing and extensive collection of mature cacti in a series of large gardens. This is very quiet road, so you can stop for photographs and to marvel at the spectacle. Not one you'll quickly forget; not usually seen by tourists

The road that passes between The Arepera and The Don Quixote bars leads us to Charco Del Paulo which is a very nice village with four bars, a supermarket and three different

points where it is possible to swim. The village welcomes naturists, so although you can dress as modestly as you wish, you may find that others don't; show respect with cameras. Accommodation at Charco del Paulo is offered by the unrivalled services of Wendy and Alan at http://www.nudelanza.com/. There are (*of course*) many fine L&W walks starting at Charco de Palo.

The road to Charco passes between Cactus fields cultivated for the cochineal beetle, used in food colouring. Close examination of the cacti, reveals white powder which is a fungus growing on the exudate of these tiny beetles. The industry once served much of the world, before being replaced by cheaper artificial colourings. However, the fashion for natural ingredients is seeing something of a revival for these ffields. Small jars of the liquid can be purchased in the Arepera Bar and a museum opposite the bar tells the whole story.

Guatiza

From Mala, continue, South, to reach Guatiza, which is a pleasant town worthy of an exploratory walk.

There is a fine church a Sociedad and Bulin's Bar, a roadside bar operated by a prestidigitationalist of the highest standard. As a new face at the bar there is a very high probability that you will be entertained with a display of slight-of-hand that is difficult to explain. There is a supermarket and opposite that a cashpoint. The village is worthy of ambulatory exploration, having a fine church and behind that a splendid Sociedad.

Teseguite

From the Guatiza roundabout do not, yet, re-join the LZ1, but to see a wonder *not of this world*, pass under it and take the service road beside it in order to turn Right towards Teseguite, and Teguise.

Teseguite is very pleasant and well worth a look, as is El Mojon, to the Right (Very nice church).

What is more important, though, is the quarry on your way there. Here pillars of Picon have been left standing and they are windswept into eccentric sculptures definitely not of this planet. You need to park on your right and admire them all.

Costa Teguise, volcanoes and some very fine Hobbit Holes.

Return to the LZ1 at Guatiza Garage and head South towards Arrecife. On the Left you see a turning for LZ34 towards costa Teguise under a very fine (*and totally pointless*) gatehouse arch, designed as a folly be Cesar Manrique. This road continues to the gentle Montana Saga and the rather more difficult to climb Montana Corona. Both of these

are a delight to ascend (*but that must be optional; this is not a walking book.*) What is essential is to park and walk around the quarry on the opposite side of the road to the montanas. This quarry is easy to drop down into and includes a range of 'hobbit houses' that in England would be kitted out and rented to tourists for £50/night.

Continue, turn right and you will see Costa Teguise. This is very much a tourist development with a few too many all-inclusive offerings, but it has a terrific range of bars, shops, markets and sea front. So, worth a look. Then take either of the available roads back to Tahiche and sanity.

Tahiche and the Foundation Cesar Manrique

Tahiche is pleasant with its own (*climbable*) mountain. As with every town on the island walk or drive the small roads away from the LZs. Of serious note is the Foundation Cesar Manrique which was his first home, donated to the state as a fabulously eccentric curiosity. Indeed, this may be the single most eccentric of his residences. The rooms were created by cutting tunnels between lava bubble caves and it must be seen to be believed. *Honestly - not to be missed.*

Also in Tahiche, off to your Left, is the Al Jibe bar and micro-brewery, which serves particularly fine cuisine, albeit at commensurately high prices.

Arrecife

The LZ1 brings us back to Arrecife.

Opposite the Gran Hotel is the Sociedad, offering fine drinks and food at very modest prices. The water front is varied and fun. The sea and sand are inviting. Towards the Northern end there is a Charco (sea water lake) with fine bars and another Sociedad. Further North is the Marina.

This is a fine town and as a capital city about as splendid as such a place can be. Cross over the Circumvolution road and head for the town where parking is not difficult; for a formal parking spot there is always the huge carpark under the tower-block Gran Hotel. There are endless shops and bars if you like such things and a few marvels that are a bit of a must:

1)   Castillo de San Gabrielle is a fine castle on a small island linked by two bridges to the centre of Arrecife. On foot, you pass over the Puente de las Bolas drawbridge. Built originally as a wooden fortress, it proved insufficient and was burnt down by Berber pirates. It was rebuilt in stone in the 16th Century. The fortress is now a National Historic Monument, with views over the city and the Atlantic Ocean.

Open: Tuesday to Friday from 10.00 to 13.00 hrs and from 16.00 to 19.00 hrs
       Saturdays from 10.00 to 13.00 hrs.

2) Castillo de San Jose. The castle was a very serious defensive point against pirates, and is a fine building. It now contains the International Museum of Contemporary Art *(if that appeals to you).* The building certainly is dramatic, and below it, down steps (with

free entry) is a very splendid Cesar Manrique restaurant viewing over the harbour. In the water are the tidally submerged horse sculptures by Jason deCaires Taylor which were formerly displayed in the tidal Thames.

3)   Oil drum boats. To the North of the Castillo de San Jose a pedestrian walkway takes you right past the manufacturer and custodian of these remarkable little boats, which are sailed at festivals. Each is manufactured out of the steel from just one oil drum. Rarely discovered by tourists.

4)   Very extensive sand beach (clothed).

From here, your tour is complete and my work: done!

Of course there are many other wonders on this island and a lifetime would not leave you feeling that you'd seen it all. Email me about what I have missed.

And to read further, see:

https://www.goodreads.com/author/list/2414699.Neil_Wheeler

Printed in Great Britain
by Amazon

70365925R00015